STEM IN THE REAL WORLD

ENVIRONMENTAL ENGINEERING IN THE REAL WORLD

by Angie Smibert

Content Consultant
Paige J. Novak, Professor
Department of Civil, Environmental,
and Geo Engineering
University of Minnesota

Core Library
An Imprint of Abdo Publishing
abdopublishing.com

abdopublishing.com

Published by Abdo Publishing, a division of ABDO, PO Box 398166, Minneapolis, Minnesota 55439. Copyright © 2017 by Abdo Consulting Group, Inc. International copyrights reserved in all countries. No part of this book may be reproduced in any form without written permission from the publisher. Core Library™ is a trademark and logo of Abdo Publishing.

Printed in the United States of America, North Mankato, Minnesota
092016
012017

THIS BOOK CONTAINS
RECYCLED MATERIALS

Cover Photo: Edwin Tuyay/Bloomberg/Getty Images
Interior Photos: Edwin Tuyay/Bloomberg/Getty Images, 1; Jake May/The Flint Journal/AP Images, 4; Jake May/The Flint Journal-MLive.com/AP Images, 6; Huntstock/Science Source, 9; Bettmann/Getty Images, 12, 18, 45; Sergey Dzyuba/Shutterstock Images, 14; Oxford Science Archive/Print Collector/Getty Images, 16; NASA, 20; EPA, 22; Pablo Martinez Monsivais/AP Images, 24, 43; Spencer Sutton/Science Source, 26; David Hay Jones/Science Source, 29; Luciano Mortula/Shutterstock Images, 32; Geraldo Caso/AFP/Getty Images, 35; Paul Rapson/Science Source, 37; Monica Schroeder/Science Source, 39

Editor: Arnold Ringstad
Series Designer: Ryan Gale

Publisher's Cataloging-in-Publication Data

Names: Smibert, Angie, author.
Title: Environmental engineering in the real world / by Angie Smibert.
Description: Minneapolis, MN : Abdo Publishing, 2017. | Series: STEM in the real
    world | Includes bibliographical references and index.
Identifiers: LCCN 2016945468 | ISBN 9781680784787 (lib. bdg.) |
    ISBN 9781680798630 (ebook)
Subjects: LCSH: Environmental engineering--Juvenile literature.
Classification: DDC 628--dc23
LC record available at http://lccn.loc.gov/2016945468

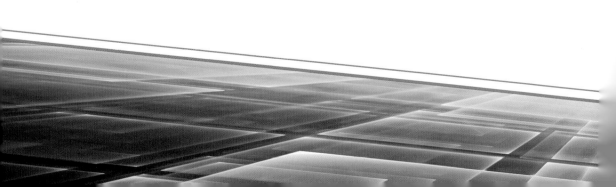

CONTENTS

CHAPTER ONE

NOT SAFE TO DRINK

It was a warm day in September 2015. Environmental engineer Marc Edwards held two bottles of tap water. The first was labeled "Detroit." The second said "Flint." Its water was brown and cloudy. This water was flowing into the homes of Flint, Michigan. It was making people sick. Edwards and his team announced what many people already suspected. Flint had a serious lead problem.

Edwards shows the difference between water from Flint and water from Detroit.

Doctors performed blood tests on the people of Flint to check for lead poisoning.

More than 10 percent of the homes he studied had lead levels above the legal limits. One house even had 1,000 times more lead than allowed. The child living there was suffering from lead poisoning.

How did this happen? In April 2014, the city of Flint changed its drinking water source. It had been using the system of Detroit, Michigan. Now it used

the Flint River. The river water was corrosive. It ate away at the pipes. Many of these pipes are made of lead. Soon after the switch, the people of Flint noticed changes. The water coming out of their taps was brown. It also smelled. Some people complained of itchy skin. Others started getting sick.

The government told residents the water was fine. But many residents did not believe it. A local doctor tested many children. She found high levels of lead. One of the children's mothers contacted Edwards. She had read about similar work he had done elsewhere. The concerned mother sent his lab a sample of her water.

Lead Poisoning

Lead is a naturally occurring element. Humans have used it for centuries to make many things. Bullets, batteries, and pipes contain lead. It was also added to gasoline and paint in the past. But lead is toxic to people and animals. One of the most common causes of lead poisoning is from lead paint. The United States banned lead in household paint in 1978. Children living in older homes can get sick from eating lead paint chips or dust.

Edwards discovered it had very high lead levels. It was the worst he had ever seen.

Over the next year, Edwards and his team tested more water samples. The study brought national attention to Flint's lead problem. Edwards's work helped spotlight the issue of unsafe water.

What Is Environmental Engineering?

Environmental engineers use technology to fix or prevent environmental problems. The environment is the world in which we live. It includes both living and nonliving things. People need clean water, air, and soil to stay healthy.

IN THE REAL WORLD

Other Contaminants

Environmental engineers test drinking water for more than lead. In the United States, the Safe Drinking Water Act sets maximum levels for more than 90 contaminants. Some of the maximum levels are zero. Drinking water cannot have any viruses, arsenic, or uranium. Community water systems must give consumers a report every year on how clean their drinking water is.

Testing water for pollution is an important part of environmental engineering.

Environmental engineers protect humans from pollution. They also help protect the environment from people.

Environmental engineering is a diverse field. Some engineers focus on drinking water. Some specialize in a type of pollution. Or they might find ways to combat climate change. Climate change is a long-term shift in Earth's temperature. It is caused by some kinds of air pollutants. Environmental engineers make our lives and environment cleaner.

In articles and interviews, engineer Larry Clark has discussed the lessons that should be learned from the Flint water crisis:

> If all of the technical factors had been considered prior to the switch in water supplies being made, the outcome could have been very different. . . . I wonder how many of the individuals who made those bad decisions were professional engineers, licensed plumbers, or water-treatment specialists? The involvement of such professionals might have made a difference.
>
> Clearly, elected and appointed officials without the technical training/knowledge in those areas should consult with professionals before making these types of decisions. . . . After all of the negative press associated with Flint, I can't imagine another jurisdiction making this kind of a change without consulting a variety of qualified professionals and relying on their expertise going forward.

Source: Jessica Lyons Hardcastle. "How to Prevent Another Flint Water Crisis." Environmental Leader. *Environmental Leader*, February 1, 2016. Web. Accessed June 27, 2016.

Point of View

Clark says that engineers should be more involved in decisions that involve water safety. Why does he say this? Read back through the chapter. Do you agree? Why or why not?

NEW PROFESSION, ANCIENT ROOTS

The term *environmental engineer* was first used in the 1960s. But engineers have been helping protect public health for thousands of years. People have always needed safe water. Engineers helped bring drinking water into cities. And as cities grew, people saw the effects of pollution. Engineers helped lessen these effects.

The ancient Romans built large structures called aqueducts to carry water from place to place.

Roman aqueducts can still be seen today in many places, including Spain.

From Ancient Rome to the 1800s

Engineers in ancient Rome understood the need for safe drinking water. They built aqueducts and sewers throughout Roman territory. The first aqueduct was built in 312 BCE. By 97 CE, the city of Rome itself had nine aqueducts. They brought fresh water from the mountains into the city. This system included 220 miles (350 km) of pipes. Many Roman aqueducts are still standing today.

The Roman Empire fell in 476 CE. Much of its engineering knowledge was lost for centuries. In many cities, people disposed of waste in rivers. People also drank from these rivers. These practices allowed illnesses to spread. Diseases such as cholera and typhoid were everywhere. A Roman citizen in 30 CE had a longer life span than a person living 1,000 years later.

By the 1800s, people in Europe began to see the connection between polluted water and disease. In 1849 a famous study in London, England, traced

Pollution in London's important Thames River became notorious in the mid-1850s.

the cause of a cholera outbreak. London's water system was responsible. The city began work on a sewer system in 1858. This reduced many waterborne diseases. Other cities soon built sewer systems too.

The Environmental Movement

After World War II (1939–1945), pollution disasters grabbed public attention. They showed how people were harming the environment. For instance, smog killed 20 people in a Pennsylvania mill town in 1948. Debris

IN THE REAL WORLD
The Great Stink

In the hot summer of 1858, the Thames River stank of human waste. The river runs through London. London is one of the biggest cities in the world. In the mid-1800s, Londoners dumped their sewage into the river. They got their drinking water from it as well. This caused dysentery, typhoid, and cholera epidemics. These diseases spread through unclean water. They killed thousands of people. In that summer, the smell of the river was worse than ever. The government finally had civil engineer Joseph Bazalgette build a sewer system. He designed 82 miles (132 km) of new sewers.

Oil pollution resulted in debris in the Cuyahoga River catching fire several times.

in Ohio's polluted Cuyahoga River caught fire in 1969. A neighborhood in Niagara Falls, New York, was shown to be polluted by chemical waste in the 1970s. During this period, books such as Rachel Carson's *Silent Spring* educated people about harm to the environment.

In the United States, environmental incidents led to the creation of the Environmental Protection

Agency (EPA) in 1970. The government passed new laws to protect the environment. Those laws limited air and water pollution. They ensured safe drinking water. They also protected wildlife. Scientists made sure businesses followed the new rules. Engineers studied the environmental impact of every new construction project. Modern environmental engineering was born.

By the early 2000s, people had come to realize how humanity had affected the planet.

Silent Spring

Rachel Carson published the book *Silent Spring* in 1962. She wrote about how a pesticide, DDT, was poisoning the environment. DDT was used on farms and public lands after World War II. It killed mosquitoes, stopping these insects from spreading diseases. It worked very well. But it also had unexpected negative effects. Carson explained how the pesticide built up in birds. It made their eggshells thinner. The eggs cracked easily. The baby birds did not survive. She wrote of a silent spring without birds because of DDT. The book led to government investigations of pesticides. It helped inspire the formation of the EPA in 1970.

In the 1960s, photos of Earth from space showed the planet's fragility and helped inspire the environmental movement.

Today's environmental engineers still work to prevent and treat pollution. But they also build sustainably, explore alternative energy sources, and combat climate change.

In this excerpt from Rachel Carson's *Silent Spring*, she describes the effects of harmful chemicals on the environment:

> *For each of us, as for the robin in Michigan or the salmon in the Miramichi, this is a problem of ecology, of interrelationships, of interdependence. We poison the caddis flies in a stream and the salmon runs dwindle and die. We poison the gnats in a lake and the poison travels from link to link of the food chain and soon the birds of the lake margins become its victims. We spray our elms and the following springs are silent of robin song, not because we sprayed the robins directly but because the poison traveled, step by step, through the now familiar elm leaf-earthworm-robin cycle. These are matters of record, observable, part of the visible world around us. They reflect the web of life—or death—that scientists know as ecology.*

Source: Rachel Carson. Silent Spring. New York: Mariner, 2002. Print. 189.

What's the Big Idea?

Take a close look at this passage. How can pesticides have unintended consequences? What examples of this does the author give?

ENVIRONMENTAL ENGINEERING TODAY

Environmental engineers work in a variety of places. Many environmental engineers and scientists work for the government. They join agencies such as the EPA. Other environmental engineers work for private companies. Some do research and teach at universities. Most tend to focus on a specific area, resource, or type of pollution.

An EPA team examines the Animas River in Colorado.

Northeast High School
Oakland Park, Florida

InvenTeams™

LEMELS●N·MIT

High school students demonstrate a bicycle-powered water filter system to President Barack Obama.

To become an environmental engineer, a person needs a bachelor's degree in engineering. Different universities have different names for the program. The degree may be called environmental or civil engineering. Interested students in high school

should take math and science classes. For instance, a university might require algebra, geometry, precalculus, biology, chemistry, and physics. Each university's website includes information about what classes a high school student should take.

It is also important for environmental engineers to have good communication skills. They may have to share ideas with other engineers. They may work with the government to ensure environmental laws are being followed. They may talk to communities about local environmental problems and solutions.

Water

Clean and plentiful water is essential for life. Like Marc Edwards, an environmental engineer might focus on drinking water. This water comes from lakes, rivers, or underground sources. It must be treated and processed to make it safe to drink. An environmental engineer may test drinking water for pollutants. He or she might run a city's water treatment plant.

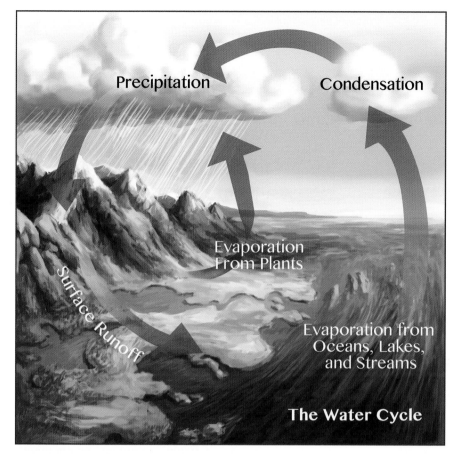

Precipitation

Condensation

Evaporation From Plants

Evaporation from Oceans, Lakes, and Streams

Surface Runoff

The Water Cycle

The Water Cycle

Earth's water is always in motion. A drop of water may evaporate from the ocean, fall as rain over the mountains, and then run into a lake. Study the chart above. How might pollution from surface runoff make its way into drinking water?

There, environmental engineers clean the city's drinking water.

Environmental engineers are also involved in other aspects of water science. They may monitor

water underground and in lakes, rivers, oceans, and wetlands. They may look for new water sources or develop new technologies to purify water. For instance, an environmental engineer might work at a desalination plant. These facilities remove salt from seawater. This makes the water drinkable.

Waste Management

The world has more than 7 billion people. Together, all those people produce a lot of waste. This can take the form of wastewater or solid waste. Wastewater

IN THE REAL WORLD
Superfund Cleanup

From 1952 to 1979, a company called Marathon made batteries at a site in Cold Spring, New York. The factory's wastewater contaminated the Hudson River and nearby wetlands with cadmium. This toxic element is used in batteries. The cadmium also spread to a wildlife sanctuary. In the early 1980s, the EPA added the Marathon site to the Superfund list. This is a list of contaminated places in the United States. Once a site is listed, the EPA oversees the cleanup process. In this case, the cleanup included digging up contaminated sediment. The buildings were demolished, and the wetlands were restored.

includes sewage from buildings. It may come from homes, businesses, or schools. It travels down drains and through pipes to wastewater treatment plants. There it is cleaned and processed so it will not harm the environment. The treated water returns to lakes or rivers.

Solid waste can include trash and any other kind of discarded material. Environmental engineers work in wastewater treatment plants, landfills, and recycling operations. They may clean up contamination from waste. They may also find new ways to recycle or reuse it, including reusing wastewater for irrigation or even drinking water.

Air Quality

Factories, cars, and farming release many substances into the air. These can affect not only human health but also the climate. For instance, most spray cans once used chemicals called chlorofluorocarbons (CFCs). When CFCs were released into the air, they damaged Earth's ozone layer. This layer of the

Researchers release balloons carrying scientific instruments into the atmosphere to study the ozone layer.

atmosphere protects Earth's surface from some of the sun's harmful rays.

Environmental engineers monitor emissions in the air. Some design new technology to clean up

air pollution. Engineers also study how air pollution moves in the atmosphere. Studying the effects of CFCs led to them being banned in the 1970s. The ozone layer has begun to recover.

Renewable Energy

The world's supply of fossil fuels, such as oil and coal, is limited. Burning fossil fuels also contributes to pollution and climate change. Environmental engineers work with people in other fields to explore renewable energy. These energy sources are not depleted when they are used. These resources

Algal Biofuel

Biofuel can be made from several sources. They include plant oils, animal fat, and algae. Algae show great promise. They grow quickly. Some species can double their population in a single day. And algae yield more oil than plants such as soybeans. Algae are being grown in vast open ponds and in photobioreactors. Photobioreactors grow algae in rows of plastic tubes exposed to sunlight. Algae also remove carbon dioxide from the air as they grow. They can be used to treat wastewater.

include the sun and the wind, as well as biofuels from waste, algae, and plants.

Many of the problems environmental engineers deal with are related to pollution from burning fossil fuels. Switching to renewable energy sources can help keep these problems from happening in the first place.

FURTHER EVIDENCE

Chapter Three covers several fields in which environmental engineers work. What were some of those areas? Which ones sounded most interesting to you? Explore the site below. Does the career information support what you've read in this chapter? Does it give you more options?

Engineer Your Life: Environmental Engineering
mycorelibrary.com/environmental-engineering

FUTURE CHALLENGES

I n the future, the world's population and cities will continue to grow. More and more countries will develop. Natural resources will continue to be depleted, and the climate will continue changing. For environmental engineers, the future is full of challenges. Some of the major challenges include supplying clean water and reusing water.

Supplying huge cities with clean water is one of the jobs of environmental engineers.

Climate Change

Earth's average temperature has risen 1.4 degrees Fahrenheit (0.8°C) over the past century. If it rises much more, the effects of global warming will become very serious. Rising temperatures cause changes in our climate. They could trigger floods and droughts. They could melt sea ice, causing sea levels to rise. Some climate change can be due to natural causes, such as volcanic eruptions. But nearly all scientists agree the current warming trend is caused by human activities. Human activities release gases into the atmosphere. One of these is carbon dioxide. Most of it is released by burning fossil fuels. These fuels include coal, oil, and natural gas.

Clean Water

Developed countries, such as the United States, usually have clean water available. But in developing countries, supplying clean water can be a major challenge. These places often lack the money to build large water treatment plants.

One issue in these areas involves fluoride. In developed countries, small amounts of fluoride are often added to drinking water. This chemical helps strengthen teeth. But in some developing countries,

Engineers developed a special straw that filters water as people drink through it.

too much fluoride is naturally present. It can be harmful to teeth and bones.

Scientists working in Africa are finding ways to cheaply filter water to make it safer to drink. They are using local materials, such as charred bone and wood. They work with people in Ethiopia to provide clean water. In 2012 the United Nations estimated 884 million people around the world lacked nearby safe drinking water. Environmental engineers are finding ways to reduce that number.

Water Reuse

Today's environmental engineers are finding ways to reuse water. In many parts of the world, severe droughts leave areas low on water supplies. The state of California has been hit especially hard by droughts.

One way to reduce the impact of droughts is to recycle water. Engineers are finding ways to treat wastewater. It can then be used in farm fields, toilets, and industrial processes. This requires less treatment than it would if the water were used for drinking.

Processing wastewater is one step in efficient water reuse.

When water is recycled, less water needs to be taken from lakes, rivers, and underground sources. People can stretch low water supplies further.

Climate Change

Some environmental engineers are developing new ways to fight climate change. Burning fossil fuels usually releases carbon dioxide into the atmosphere, warming the planet. But the gas can instead be captured and stored. It can be held underground in caverns or within rock formations. Engineers are working on ways to make this storage safe and secure. By preventing the release of carbon dioxide, they can slow the process of climate change. Environmental engineers are also working on new forms of renewable energy. One of these new developments involves using wastewater to make fuels.

Restoring Urban Infrastructure

The infrastructure of many developed countries is aging. Infrastructure includes systems such as roads,

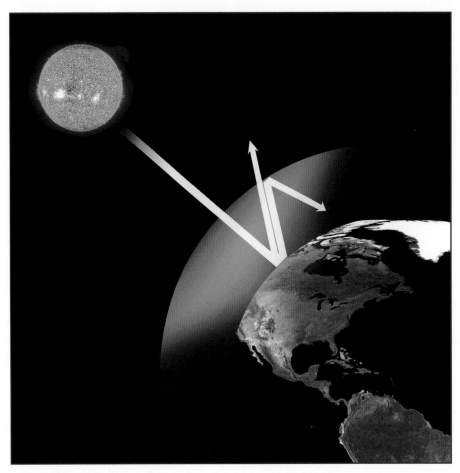

The Greenhouse Effect

Greenhouse gases include carbon dioxide and methane. They trap the sun's radiation in the atmosphere. This warms Earth's surface, much as the glass in a greenhouse helps warm the space inside. What might happen if we had more greenhouse gases in the atmosphere? What might happen if we had less?

dams, water pipes, and sewers. The lead pipes of Flint are just one example. Cities around the world are outgrowing their infrastructure. Engineers will be

Green Roofs of Chicago

In 2005 the city of Chicago, Illinois, started a program to encourage green roofs. Green roofs are roofs covered with soil and plants. A waterproof lining protects the original roof. The city began the program as a way to control storm water runoff. Rainwater was flooding the streets and sewers. Green roofs absorb and clean the rainwater. A green roof has other benefits as well. It improves air quality, cools the building, and reduces noise. The plants help take carbon dioxide out of the atmosphere. By 2010 Chicago had more than 500 green roofs.

challenged to replace or fix buildings, roads, pipes, and power grids sustainably. Environmental engineers have a big role in this. They will work with other engineers to come up with innovative solutions that protect human health and the environment.

These are just a few of the challenges tomorrow's engineers will face. Environmental engineers will be needed to ensure we have safe water, air, and land. They will clean up hazardous sites, explore new energy

sources, and combat climate change. Environmental engineers will be essential in building a sustainable future for us all.

EXPLORE ONLINE

Chapter Four mentions climate change as a major environmental engineering challenge. Climate change is already affecting sea ice, sea levels, and global temperature. The website below lets you see these effects. How will rising sea levels impact the coast of Florida or the city of Amsterdam in the Netherlands? How has Arctic sea ice changed since 1979? How much of the world is warmer than average in the 2000s?

NASA Climate Time Machine
mycorelibrary.com/environmental-engineering

FAST FACTS

- Environmental engineers use science and technology to solve or prevent environmental problems.
- The profession grew out of a need for safe drinking water.
- The ancient Romans built aqueducts to carry clean drinking water from distant sources into cities.
- After Rome fell, a lack of clean water and sanitation led to many disease outbreaks.
- In the 1800s, people in Europe discovered that unclean water is responsible for disease. They launched programs to build new sewers to keep cities cleaner.
- In the United States, many environmental protection laws were passed in the 1970s. This created a demand for environmental engineers.
- Environmental engineers often focus on protecting a particular resource, such as air or water, or study a particular type of pollution or waste.

Northeast High School
Oakland Park, Florida

InvenTeams™

LEMELSON-MIT

- Climate change is the overall average rise in Earth's temperature caused by human activity. It is one of many challenges facing environmental engineers.
- Today's environmental engineers are studying ways to bring clean drinking water to more people. They are also finding ways to recycle existing water supplies.

Surprise Me

Chapter Four talks about climate change. After reading this chapter, what facts about climate change surprised you? Why did you find them surprising? Write a few sentences about each fact.

Say What?

Studying environmental engineering can mean learning new scientific and engineering vocabulary. Find five words in this book whose meanings you don't know. Use a dictionary or encyclopedia to find out what they mean. Then write the meanings in your own words, and use each word in a new sentence.

You Are There

Imagine you are starting the first day of your new job as an environmental engineer. What are you working on? Write an e-mail to your friends and family describing your job. Be sure to add plenty of detail.

Take a Stand

Chapter Two discusses the negative impact that people can have on the environment, including contamination by companies. When this kind of contamination occurs, who do you think should be responsible for the cleanup? Be sure to give reasons to back up your opinion.

GLOSSARY

aqueduct
a structure that carries water over land

climate
the usual weather conditions over a long period of time in a particular place or region

contaminate
to make dangerous or dirty by adding something harmful or undesirable

corrosive
causing damage to metal

emissions
gases released into the air

environment
the natural and human-created world around us

epidemic
the spread of a disease that affects a large number of people

pesticide
a chemical used to kill pests

photobioreactor
a piece of equipment in which algae can be grown in a controlled environment

smog
a mix of fog and pollution that can be dangerous to human health

LEARN MORE

Books

Kallio, Jamie. *12 Things to Know about Climate Change.* North Mankato, MN: 12-Story Library, 2015.

Rowell, Rebecca. *Rachel Carson Sparks the Environmental Movement.* Minneapolis, MN: Abdo Publishing, 2016.

Websites

To learn more about STEM in the Real World, visit **booklinks.abdopublishing.com**. These links are routinely monitored and updated to provide the most current information available.

Visit **mycorelibrary.com** for free additional tools for teachers and students.

INDEX

ABOUT THE AUTHOR

Angie Smibert is the author of several young adult science fiction novels, numerous short stories, and many educational titles just like this one. She worked as a science writer for NASA, the US Department of Energy, and the EPA.

DATE DUE

			PRINTED IN U.S.A.

Face the Facts
Racism

Adrian Cooper

For information, address the publisher:
Raintree, 100 N. LaSalle, Suite 1200, Chicago, IL 60602

Design by Jamie Asher/Mayer Media
Printed and bound in China.
07 06 05 04 03
10 9 8 7 6 5 4 3 2 1

Library of Congress Cataloging-in-Publication Data

Cooper, Adrian.
  Racism / Adrian Cooper.
    v. cm. -- (Face the facts)
Contents: What is racism? -- Race and racists : what is race? -- Racism in history -- Racism in society -- Racism and you -- Experiences of racism -- Facts and figures.
  ISBN 0-7398-6434-3 (HC), 1-4109-0047-9 (Pbk.)
  1. Racism--Juvenile literature. [1. Racism.] I. Title. II. Series.
  HT1521 .C636 2003
  305.8--dc21
                              2002013050

Acknowledgments
The publishers would like to thank the following for permission to reproduce photographs:
pp. 1, 10, 12, 14, 17 AKG London; p. 5 (top), 37 David Hoffman Photo Library; p. 5 (bottom) Nick Cobbing/David Hoffman Photo Library; pp. 6–7, 32, 38, 39, 47, 48–49 Image Works/Topham Picturepoint; p. 7 Ancient Art and Architecture Collection; pp. 7, 15, 19 (top), 28 (top) Prosport/Topham Picturepoint; p. 9 Ronnie Kaufman/Corbis Stock Market; pp.16, 28 (bottom), Reuters/Popperfoto; p. 19 (bottom) Robert W. Kelly/Timepix/Rex Features; p. 21 Mirek Towski/Rex Features; p. 22 Camera Press; pp. 24, 25, 30 Nils Jorgensen/Rex Features; p. 27 Steve Chenn/Corbis; p. 31 Terry Thompson/Rex Features; p. 34 MXL/Rex Features; p. 36 Dita Alangkara/Associated Press; p. 36 Santiago Lyon/Associated Press; p. 41 PA/John Stillwell/Topham Picturepoint; p. 43 (top) Marcus Zeffler/Rex Features; p. 43 (bottom) Mike Hutchings/Reuters/Popperfoto; pp. 44–45 Richard Young/Rex Features; p. 50 John Birdsall Photography.

Cover photograph: Format/Ulrike Press

Some words are shown in bold, **like this.** You can find out what they mean by looking in the Glossary.